DJUSD
Public Schools
Library Protection Act 1998

SPORTS GREAT
OREL
HERSHISER

—Sports Great Books—

Sports Great Jim Abbott (ISBN 0-89490-395-0)

Sports Great Charles Barkley (ISBN 0-89490-386-1)

Sports Great Larry Bird (ISBN 0-89490-368-3)

Sports Great Bobby Bonilla (ISBN 0-89490-417-5)

Sports Great Will Clark (ISBN 0-89490-390-X)

Sports Great Roger Clemens (ISBN 0-89490-284-9)

Sports Great John Elway (ISBN 0-89490-282-2)

Sports Great Patrick Ewing (ISBN 0-89490-369-1)

Sports Great Orel Hershiser (ISBN 0-89490-389-6)

Sports Great Bo Jackson (ISBN 0-89490-281-4)

Sports Great Magic Johnson (Revised and Expanded) (ISBN 0-89490-348-9)

Sports Great Michael Jordan (ISBN 0-89490-370-5)

Sports Great Kevin Mitchell (ISBN 0-89490-388-8)

Sports Great Joe Montana (ISBN 0-89490-371-3)

Sports Great Hakeem Olajuwon (ISBN 0-89490-372-1)

Sports Great Kirby Puckett (ISBN 0-89490-392-6)

Sports Great Jerry Rice (ISBN 0-89490-419-1)

Sports Great Cal Ripken, Jr. (ISBN 0-89490-387-X)

Sports Great David Robinson (ISBN 0-89490-373-X)

Sports Great Nolan Ryan (ISBN 0-89490-394-2)

Sports Great Barry Sanders (ISBN 0-89490-418-3)

Sports Great Darryl Strawberry (ISBN 0-89490-291-1)

Sports Great Isiah Thomas (ISBN 0-89490-374-8)

Sports Great Herschel Walker (ISBN 0-89490-207-5)

SPORTS GREAT
OREL
HERSHISER

Ron Knapp

—Sports Great Books—

Enslow Publishers, Inc.

44 Fadem Road	PO Box 38
Box 699	Aldershot
Springfield, NJ 07081	Hants GU12 6BP
USA	UK

Library of Congress Cataloging-in-Publication Data

Knapp, Ron.

    Sports great Orel Hershiser / Ron Knapp.
        p. cm. — (Sports great books)
    Includes index.
    Summary: A biography of the pitcher for the Los Angeles Dodgers whose
achievements have earned him a Cy Young award and a World Series championship.
    ISBN 0-89490-389-6
    1. Hershiser, Orel—Juvenile literature. 2. Baseball players—United
States—Biography—Juvenile literature. [1. Hershiser, Orel. 2. Baseball players.] I. Title.
II. Series.
GV865.H46K58 1993
796.357'092—dc20
[B]   92-11329
                                             CIP
                                             AC

Printed in the United States of America

10 9 8 7 6 5 4

Photo credits: Atlanta Braves, p. 33; BGSU Public Relations Office, p. 19; Kansas
City Royals, p. 37; Los Angeles Dodgers, pp. 8, 20, 23; Mitchell Layton
Photography, pp. 26, 28, 31, 35, 40, 42, 49, 53, 55, 58; New York Convention and
Visitors Bureau, p. 15; Oakland Athletics, pp. 10, 12; San Francisco Giants, p. 46.

Cover Photo: AP/Wide World Photos.

Contents

Chapter 1 7

Chapter 2 14

Chapter 3 22

Chapter 4 30

Chapter 5 39

Chapter 6 51

Career Statistics 60

Where to Write 61

Index 62

Chapter 1

More than 55,000 fans were crowded into the Oakland Coliseum. They wanted to see the Los Angeles Dodgers face the Oakland Athletics in the fifth game of the 1988 World Series. Millions more people were watching the baseball championship on TV.

The series now stood at 3–1 in favor of the Dodgers. One more win, and Los Angeles would be the world champs. Once again Orel Hershiser would be pitching.

Hershiser had shut out the Athletics in the second game of the series. The only Oakland player who got a hit was Dave Parker. He had three hits—all of them on singles. The Dodger pitcher had gotten some key hits as well. No one had scored until the third inning when Hershiser came home to score the first run. In the fourth inning, Hershiser doubled in Alfredo Griffin to make the score 6–0. Two innings later he got another double. The game ended 6–0.

In the first inning of this fifth game, Mickey Hatcher's home run with Franklin Stubbs on base gave the Dodgers a 2–0 lead. The A's finally scored on Hershiser in the third,

Orel's hitting helped the Dodgers against the Oakland A's.

when Stan Javier's sacrifice fly brought in Carney Lansford. In the next inning, Mike Davis cracked a two-run homer, and the Dodgers were up 4–1. Rick Dempsey doubled in Davis to make the score 5–1 in the sixth. Hershiser knew he was hot, and he knew his team was just a few innings short of a World Series championship. To stay calm he began praying, talking to himself, and even softly singing as he sat in the dugout.

Going into the eighth inning, LA still led 5–1. The Athletics hadn't had a hit since the third inning. The Oakland players tried to upset Hershiser by stepping out of the batter's box just as he was about to pitch. That made Hershiser mad, and more determined than ever to get the batters out.

But Hershiser walked Tony Phillips, who then went to second on a ground out. Next Javier singled him home to make it 5–2. Rickey Henderson walked on four pitches. Then Hershiser threw a wild pitch, and the runners advanced again. Finally it looked like Hershiser was beatable. In fact, he looked rattled. Dodger manager Tommy Lasorda was afraid his pitcher was losing his stuff. The manager ordered his relief pitchers to warm up in the bull pen.

"I was running out of gas," Orel later admitted. The Oakland fans cheered as Jose Canseco walked up to the plate. Nobody had to remind Hershiser that Canseco had hit a grand slam home run in the first game. Another homer now, and the game would be tied.

Canseco fouled off three pitches. Then Dodger catcher Dempsey called time and walked to the mound. He told Orel that Canseco was probably expecting a fastball over the plate. Why not trick him with another pitch? Hershiser followed his catcher's advice. He surprised Canseco with an inside fastball that the batter popped up. The Athletics now had two outs.

Jose Canseco's grand slam home run gave the Oakland A's a big lead in the first game of the 1988 World Series.

Next Hershiser had to face Dave Parker—the only Athletic to get a hit in the second game. A homer would still tie the game. After working the count to 1–1, Parker struck out on a pair of curveballs. The eighth inning ended with the Dodgers still ahead 5–2. Hershiser walked off the field and held up three fingers. Three more outs and the World Series would be over.

The Dodgers failed to score in the last inning. Then Mark McGwire led off for Oakland in the bottom of the ninth. The A's fans jumped to their feet when McGwire blasted a shot deep to center field. But John Shelby caught it in front of the wall for the first out. Next Hershiser struck out Ron Hassey on three straight pitches. The last hope for Oakland was Lansford. He hit the ball hard to Alfredo Griffin and managed to beat out an infield single. The Athletics now had a man on with two outs. They were just three runs down.

Hershiser's first three pitches to Phillips were balls. Meanwhile Lansford was stealing second and third bases. The Dodgers weren't paying any attention to him. They were concentrating on Phillips. If Hershiser walked him, the tying run would be at bat. Phillips watched the next pitch, which came in right over the plate for strike one. Phillips was still watching when Hershiser pitched another strike. Now the count was full. Hershiser fired again. This time Phillips swung—and missed. The 1988 World Series was all over, leaving Los Angeles the world champs.

Hershiser was at the center of the Dodger celebration on the field. But his eyes were on the stands, looking for his wife Jamie. When he finally found her, she was smiling and cheering. Orel smiled back. Then he raised both fists and yelled. It had been quite a year. Not only had he pitched the Dodgers to a National League pennant and a World Series victory, he had also finished the regular

Mark McGwire's long fly ball was caught by John Selby in the ninth inning of Game 5.

season by pitching 59 consecutive scoreless innings. Nobody in the history of major league baseball had ever done that!

Orel's Dodger teammate Kirk Gibson said, "It may be that no pitcher in history stayed in that kind of groove so long or so well."

Chapter 2

Orel Hershiser didn't look like a superstar athlete. "Let's face it," he said. "I'm just a pale guy with glasses, long arms and a sunken chest. I look like I never lifted a weight. I look like I work in a flour factory."

Orel may not have looked like a big star, but he had loved sports ever since he was a child. He was born September 16, 1958, in Buffalo, New York. His parents, Orel and Millie, named him Orel Leonard Hershiser IV. He shared the name with his father and grandfather. To avoid confusion he was called "Little O," and his dad was called "Big O."

Little O was a fine athlete, though always small for his age. He played many different sports, but baseball was his favorite. The Hershiser family moved to Southfield, Michigan, about the time he started school. It was there he first played tee ball—a game for small children in which the ball is hit off a tee, instead of being pitched.

By the time he was seven years old, Orel was one of the best baseball players on his team. But the next summer he didn't play nearly as well because it was hard for him to see the ball. After a trip to the eye doctor, he got his first pair of glasses. Once again he was one of the top players on his team.

When he was eight, Little O competed in the 1967 Personna Baseball Contest. He won this competition by hitting, running, and throwing farther than anybody else in Southfield. That qualified him for the national finals at Yankee Stadium in New York City. When he walked into the beautiful old stadium, he was amazed by its size. He wondered how anybody could ever hit a home run over the outfield wall. Little O, of course, wasn't strong enough to hit a home run. But he did well enough in the finals to win a third-place trophy.

After that day at Yankee Stadium, Orel had no doubts about his future. He wanted to be a major league baseball

Orel stood on the field at Yankee Stadium when he was only eight years old.

player. When he grew up he wanted to play in places like Yankee Stadium.

While Orel was growing up, he couldn't get enough of baseball. On the day of a big game he liked to put on his uniform early, then lie in his bedroom, listening to records. That helped him get fired up so that he would play his best.

When Orel was twelve, the Hershisers moved from Southfield to Toronto, Canada—where he learned to play ice hockey. When his family moved to Cherry Hill, New Jersey, a year later, he played both sports.

Orel's parents always encouraged their children to be active in sports. They helped organize the Little League in Buffalo, where Orel first learned to play. They raked the playing fields, organized the teams, coached, umpired, and sold snacks at the concession stand. Years later Orel said his father was the one who taught him to be a great competitor. His father convinced him to play hard and never give up.

Mr. Hershiser had a good job with a printing company and was transferred many times to different offices. That's why the family moved from Buffalo to Southfield to Cherry Hill. Orel, his brothers Gordie and Judd, and his sister Katie were never allowed to take it easy. All of them had chores to do. Instead of watching TV cartoons on Saturday mornings, the Hershiser children had to clean the house. They kept working until the job was finished. If they complained, their father told them the only way to achieve their goals was to work. He wanted his children to get used to working hard while they were still young.

When Orel was in high school, he earned spending money by working at a neighborhood gas station. But his parents always made sure he still had time for his schoolwork and sports. During the winters he continued playing ice hockey, but his favorite sport remained baseball. When he wasn't pitching he played shortstop. "I was not the best player on my team . . . ," he said, "but I loved the game and the competition."

In ninth grade Orel tried out for the varsity baseball team. But he wasn't good enough, so he was moved to the junior varsity. When he wasn't good enough for that team either, he wound up on the freshman team. The next year he earned a spot on the junior varsity team. He finally made the varsity team in eleventh grade.

Orel might not have been the best player on the varsity squad, but he did well enough to make the all-conference team when he was a senior. During summers he also competed on a team in the Babe Ruth League. When he was sixteen, he pitched a no-hitter, but the *Cherry Hill News* misspelled his name. "NERHEISER HURLS NO-HITTER" the headline read. He also excelled in ice hockey, making the Philadelphia Flyers Junior A Team as a defenseman.

After graduating from Cherry Hill High School, Orel decided to attend Bowling Green State University in Ohio. The university had both ice hockey and baseball teams. Orel's first year there was a disaster. First the baseball coach told him to give up hockey. Then, because he didn't study, he got poor grades. In fact, his grades were so low that he was ineligible to be on the baseball team. Next his girlfriend broke up with him. Everything seemed to be going wrong for Orel. By the end of his freshman year, he was failing most of his classes, and he wasn't prepared to take his final tests. He felt miserable, believing himself to be a failure.

Orel left Ohio and went home to New Jersey. He had to admit to his family that he had done poorly at college. His parents were disappointed, but they convinced him to give it another try. He returned to Bowling Green for summer school. This time he attended classes and studied. "I just matured," he said, "and really grew to have an interest in school and going to class." That summer he made the dean's list. "From then on, I was pretty much an average student."

After summer school he played baseball on a team called Adray Appliance. The team won the All American Amateur Baseball Association national championship. He had been very excited to be the starting pitcher in the title game. But he wondered if he'd ever play in a more important game. Would he ever realize his dream of playing in the major leagues?

When Orel returned to college he continued to get good grades, but he began to lose interest in sports. He was frustrated because he was still smaller than the other players. He was six feet tall, but weighed only 155 pounds. He felt like a bean pole. His teammates were bigger, faster, and stronger. When he was a sophomore he only pitched thirteen innings and didn't win a game. Most of the time at practice he didn't do anything except chase fly balls hit by the starters who were practicing their batting. "It was frustrating, but it wasn't the coach's fault," he said. "I just didn't play well enough to make the team."

But then Little O had a sudden growth spurt. By the time he was a junior, he had grown three inches and gained twenty-seven pounds. Orel now stood at six feet, three inches and weighed 182 pounds. In fact, he was taller and heavier than his father. They had to switch nicknames, with Orel becoming "Big O" and his dad, "Little O." Orel's increase in size made him much stronger, and he could throw the ball a lot harder.

Hershiser became Bowling Green's star pitcher. He threw a 2–0 no-hitter against Kent State University, even though in the first inning he hurt his arm throwing a runner out at first base. Between innings the trainer rubbed salve on the arm, and Orel was able to keep pitching. The Kent State batters

Orel was a star pitcher at Bowling Green State University.

Orel signed a contract with the Los Angeles Dodgers in 1979.

couldn't hit him. Fifteen times they grounded out. Only four of them reached base, two on walks and two on errors.

By the end of the season, Orel's record was 6–2 and his earned run average (ERA) was 2.26. That meant he only allowed a little more than two runs in each full game he pitched. In 63-⅓ innings, he gave up only 43 hits while striking out 51. He was named Bowling Green's outstanding pitcher and was selected to the all-conference team. The Los Angeles Dodgers chose him in the 1979 draft and offered him a contract to play baseball. Boyd Bartley, the Dodger scout, told him he would be sent to a minor league team in Clinton, Iowa. If he did well enough there, someday he could earn a spot on the Dodgers.

Orel was only twenty years old, and he still had another year to go at Bowling Green. But it didn't take him long to decide that he wanted to sign with the Dodgers. Ever since he had walked into Yankee Stadium he had known he wanted to be a major league ballplayer, "I want to try," he said. "I just want to try." He accepted the contract and collected a $10,000 signing bonus. Then he headed for the minor league team in Clinton.

Chapter 3

The Clinton Dodgers are a Class A league team. Players who do well here are moved up to the San Antonio Dodgers, a Double A team in Texas. The next stop is the Triple A Albuquerque Dodgers in New Mexico. If a young player does well enough in Albuquerque, he can earn a spot in the major leagues with the Los Angeles Dodgers. Playing major league ball was Orel Hershiser's goal. But it was also the goal of dozens of other players signed by the Dodgers. Most minor league players never make it to the top. Early in his career Orel was practicing on a field with sixty other young pitchers. He thought that all of them were bigger, stronger, and better than he was. He knew then it was not going to be easy to make it to the major leagues.

Hershiser joined the Clinton Dodgers late in the 1979 season. He won four games and lost none with an ERA of 2.09. He also impressed his coaches with his desire to work hard and learn all he could. When the minor league season ended, he was sent to the Arizona Instructional League for a few more weeks of practice.

Orel thought all the other Dodger prospects looked bigger and stronger than he did.

Orel's pitching continued to improve in Arizona. But he later said the most important thing he did there was spend time with his roommate Butch Wickensheimer. Butch was different from many of the other ballplayers. He didn't hang out in bars or use bad language. On the team bus while the rest of the team relaxed or talked, Butch read his Bible.

Orel had a Bible, too, but he hardly ever read it. And he only went to church on Easter and Christmas. In Arizona he began discussing religion with his roommate. Wickensheimer answered his questions and encouraged him to read the Bible. Orel wondered if he was the type of person who could be a Christian. "I liked to have fun. I liked to be giddy."

After studying the Bible and praying, Orel made his decision. "You don't have to be a wimp to be a Christian." He began to attend church and regularly study the Bible. Since then he has said his religious beliefs are the most important things in his life. They have changed the way he lives and the way he treats other people. He said his religion has given him love and compassion for all people.

Meanwhile Orel had done well enough in Clinton and Arizona to be moved to the Double A San Antonio Dodgers in 1980. The team decided to use him as a relief pitcher. Orel came in late in the games to take over for the starting pitchers who had gotten tired or weren't doing well. During his first year in San Antonio, he only started three games. His record was a disappointing 5–9 and his ERA was 3.55.

The most important thing that happened to Hershiser that year didn't have much to do with baseball. At a team party he introduced himself to a pretty girl named Jamie Byars. She thought he was kidding when he told her his name. She didn't think anybody could have a name like "Orel Hershiser." When Orel finally convinced her he wasn't joking about his name, they had a long talk.

For their first date he invited Jamie to a game. The night was cold, and she had to sit alone in the stands while Orel played. The game went into extra innings, but she stayed until the end. Soon Jamie and Orel were spending all their free time together. Just six weeks after they met, they became engaged. They were married February 7, 1981, just before Orel started spring training.

When the season began Hershiser was doing well. He had a 0.51 ERA and was leading the Texas League in saves. He told reporters he was pitching so well because he was so happy to be married to Jamie. But suddenly his great season fell apart. On a road trip he pitched just seven innings, but gave up twenty runs. Suddenly his ERA was 4.72.

Playing in the minor leagues wasn't easy. Hardly anybody made much money. And though everybody dreamed of making it to the major leagues, most players didn't. Orel and Jamie had a tough first year together. At times they were sure Orel would never make it out of the minor leagues. "When you have a bad night or a bad week," he said, "it's like your dream is over." They wondered if he should give up baseball.

Orel had one of his worst nights in El Paso, Texas, where he gave up eight runs in less than four innings. That night he decided to quit baseball and go to work for his father. He had a long talk with the team's manager, pitching coach, and trainer. They tried to convince him to stay.

Hershiser listened to the three men and agreed to keep trying. They told him he had the talent to be a major league pitcher. By the end of the season, Orel's record was 7–6. For the 1982 season he was sent to Albuquerque to the Dodgers' top minor league team.

On his new team, Orel was still used mostly as a relief pitcher. He had a 9–6 record—good enough to impress the Texas Rangers. They tried to make a trade for him, but the

Orel joined the Los Angeles Dodgers late in the 1983 season.

deal fell through. Hershiser hoped 1983 would be the year he finally would make it to the major leagues. He did very well in spring training and won the Dearie Mulvey Award as the Dodgers' top rookie prospect. When manager Tommy Lasorda decided he still wasn't ready for the big leagues, Orel was very disappointed.

In 1983 Hershiser was still a relief pitcher and still in Albuquerque. He wondered if he'd ever make it to Los Angeles. He didn't have a great year in 1983, as he went 10–8 with a 4.09 ERA. But when the minor league season was over, he finally got the call he was waiting for. The Dodgers wanted him! He spent the last few weeks of the major league season with Los Angeles. He only pitched eight innings, but Lasorda thought he might be ready. When the 1984 season started, Hershiser didn't have to go back to Albuquerque.

Orel and Jamie bought a house in Los Angeles, but they weren't confident they would be there for long. When they needed a new headboard for their bed, Orel used a curtain rod and cushions to make one himself. The Hershisers didn't want to spend a lot of money because they weren't sure how long Orel's baseball career was going to last.

Orel's rookie year got off to a poor start. After a month he had a terrible 6.20 ERA. He was doing so poorly that Jamie volunteered to help. She offered to be his catcher so he could practice at home. Since Orel was afraid to throw her a fastball, they played catch with a pair of socks.

Lasorda brought Hershiser into his office for a talk. Orel was afraid he was being sent back to Albuquerque. The manager had been watching him closely and he wasn't pleased. He didn't think Orel believed in himself, pitching as though he was afraid every hitter was going to hit a home run. Lasorda said Hershiser had a lot of talent, but that he would

Tommy Lasorda told Orel to have more confidence.

never make it with the Dodgers if he didn't start believing in himself.

The manager told Orel to be more aggressive and to take charge on the mound. He even gave him a new name—"Bulldog." Maybe hitters would not be afraid of a pitcher named "Orel," but they had to be afraid of one named "Bulldog." Lasorda told him to look batters in the eye and let them know he was going to get them out.

Orel walked out of Lasorda's office. He knew he had to prove that he deserved the nickname "Bulldog" or he might still be on his way back to the Albuquerque Dodgers. And he knew he never wanted to play baseball in Albuquerque again.

Chapter 4

Two days after his talk with Tommy Lasorda, Orel Hershiser was back on the mound. He was called out of the bull pen as a relief pitcher. "C'mon, Bulldog! You can do it, Bulldog!" Lasorda shouted from the dugout. "You're my man, Bulldog!" Orel knew this was his big chance to prove he belonged in the major leagues. For three innings he pitched against the San Francisco Giants and gave up only one run. For the first time he really felt like a bulldog. He started to believe that Lasorda was right.

From then on when he wasn't pitching, Orel sat next to Lasorda and Ron Perranoski, the pitching coach. Orel listened in as the two men sat at the end of the Dodger dugout discussing strategy. The young pitcher wanted to learn everything he could. Even though he didn't like being a relief pitcher, he never complained. Orel wanted to help the team any way he could.

Finally he got his big chance on May 26, 1984. The Dodgers had a nationally-televised game against the New York Mets. The Dodgers' starting pitcher was supposed to be

Orel pitched 33 ⅔ consecutive scoreless innings in 1984.

Jerry Reuss, but he was injured. When Orel walked into the locker room, Lasorda threw him a baseball and said, "It's your ball. You're pitching today." That was just what Orel wanted to hear.

He had never wanted to be a relief pitcher. He wanted the chance to be a starter and pitch several times to the same batters in a game. He wanted to fool them with different pitches. Orel did the job against the Mets. Even though he didn't get the win, he pitched 6-⅓ innings and only gave up one run.

Late in June, Lasorda decided that Bulldog had earned a spot as a regular starter. For the rest of the season he would start every four games. He pitched two-hitters against the Chicago Cubs and St. Louis Cardinals before shutting out the Pittsburgh Pirates. After 33-⅔ scoreless innings, he finally gave up a run when Atlanta's Dale Murphy hit a homer. That was the longest streak of scoreless innings pitched by anybody in 1984.

In his next game against the Cincinnati Reds, Hershiser was almost perfect. For seven innings he put the Reds down in order. He was two innings away from a perfect game. In the eighth inning, he got the first two batters. Four outs to go. Cincinnati's Nick Esasky took the first pitch for a ball. Orel's next two pitches missed, too. The count was 3–0. Esasky was sure he was going to get a pitch to hit, and he did. Orel sent a strike right over the plate and Esasky lined it into the outfield. Hershiser had lost his no-hitter. But he only gave up one more hit, and the Dodgers won the game 1–0. That was Orel's third two-hitter in sixteen days.

The victory over the Reds was one of eleven for the rookie Hershiser in 1984. He lost eight times and had a respectable 2.66 ERA—his best since his first year in the minors at

Dale Murphy's home run stopped Hershiser's streak of scoreless innings in 1984.

Clinton. Orel had proven that he was at his best when he was starting. His ERA for the twenty games he started was 2.19.

After the season, Orel and Jamie had their first child, a son, on November 24, 1984. The baby's great-great-grandfather was Orel Leonard Hershiser I. His great-grandfather was Orel II, his grandfather Orel III, and his father Orel IV. Jamie knew what her husband wanted the baby to be called. "If his name was Joe Smith and he wanted to name our son that, I wouldn't have thought anything of it," she said. "Let's face it, though, Orel Leonard Hershiser is a weird name." But that was the name the baby was stuck with. He became Orel V, but Jamie insisted that he be called Quinton—a name that sounds like the Latin word for "fifth."

In 1985 Hershiser's 19–3 record made him the hottest pitcher in baseball. On April 26, he threw a 2–0 one-hitter against the San Diego Padres. The only hit was Tony Gwynn's fourth-inning single. After July 7, Orel never lost a game. In fact, he was never beaten at Dodger Stadium all year. He finished the season with eleven straight victories. He was so tough that he once faced twenty-nine batters without letting any of them hit the ball out of the infield. Orel joked that having a son must have inspired him. It made him feel lucky. The only day his luck ran out was on September 16, his 27th birthday. Quinton, who was then ten months old, fell off the edge of a bed and broke his collarbone. The injury wasn't serious, but Orel and Jamie were very upset that their son had been hurt.

The next night Orel was still worrying about Quinton when he pitched against San Diego. In the first inning, he was having a tough time thinking about the game. He gave up two singles and a walk. The bases were loaded with nobody out. It was his worst start of the season. That's when Orel got mad at himself. He decided he had to concentrate on the game. He

Tony Gwynn's single spoiled a potential no-hitter by Hershiser.

knew that Jamie was taking very good care of Quinton, and he had a job to do. While the game was going on he had to set aside his emotions and do that job. He finally managed to get the batters out, after allowing only one run. He then shut down the Padres for the rest of the night, and Los Angeles won 7–1.

After the game, when he was hurrying to get home, a reporter asked him about Quinton. Tears came to his eyes and he had to walk away and quietly cry for a few minutes. He soon dressed and returned home to his wife and son. Quinton's collarbone healed, and after a few weeks the boy was fine.

During the off-season, Hershiser signed a contract that would pay him one million dollars for 1986. Two months into the season his ERA was under 2.00, but then he started giving up more runs. By the end of the season his ERA had shot up to 3.85, and he was 14–14. He had to take a paycut to $800,000 for 1987. Once again he had another .500 record, winning the same number of games he lost. His record was 16–16, but his ERA was down to 3.06. The problem was that the Dodgers weren't scoring enough runs. For the second year in a row, Los Angeles finished fourth in the National League's West Division.

The Dodgers were pleased enough with Orel's 1987 performance to raise his salary to $1.1 million. They also tried to get him some more hitting support by signing free agent sluggers Mike Davis and Kirk Gibson. If the Dodgers could score more runs and Hershiser could have another good season, maybe 1988 would be the year Los Angeles had a shot at the pennant.

But Hershiser almost didn't make it to the start of the season. Early in February he was enjoying one of his last rounds of golf before leaving for spring training. After nine holes, his stomach began to ache. By the eighteenth and last

Kirk Gibson was signed up to put power in the Dodger line up. Later he played for the Kansas City Royals.

hole, it hurt so badly he fell to his knees. His friends helped him up, but he insisted on finishing the hole. He was sure he just had a bad stomachache, but when he got home, he fainted. Jamie and his brother Gordie rushed him to the hospital. The doctors there decided it wasn't just a stomachache. The problem was his appendix, a tiny part of his small intestine. His appendix was infected, swollen, and about to rupture—or break open.

Orel was in real pain, but if Jamie and Gordie hadn't gotten him to the hospital, he could have been in real danger. A ruptured appendix is serious enough to kill a person.

Chapter 5

Orel Hershiser was lucky. He had gotten to the hospital before his appendix ruptured. And when the doctors finally removed it, they were careful not to cut through any of the muscles in his abdomen. If the muscles had been cut, it would've taken months to get back in shape. When Orel came out of the operating room, his appendix was gone and he only had a small incision on his skin to show for it.

The day after the operation, he was walking the halls of the hospital to make sure he stayed in shape. The next day he did sit-ups and jumping jacks, and ran up and down the stairs. He was determined to be ready for the 1988 season. When the Dodgers began spring training he was there.

In Hershiser's first start against the San Francisco Giants, he got a three-hit victory. During April, he won five in a row and had a 1.56 ERA. For those reasons he was named the National League Pitcher of the Month. He didn't lose until May 12 when the Pittsburgh Pirates beat the Dodgers 7–4. The whole Los Angeles team was hot. By the end of May, the

Orel worked hard to get in shape after his surgery.

Dodgers were in first place in the National League West. Halfway through the season Orel was 13–4.

In Montreal on August 30, he had a 4–0 lead going into the fifth inning. Tim Raines doubled home a run for the Expos, and then came in himself when Davey Martinez singled. But Hershiser shut out the Expos the rest of the way, and Los Angeles won 4–2.

On September 5, Orel pitched against the Atlanta Braves. The Dodgers scored two runs in the top of the first inning. Then in the bottom of the first, with two outs, Atlanta's Gerald Perry doubled. Dale Murphy was the next batter, and it took Orel a while to get him out. Murphy finally struck out on a 3–2 pitch, stranding Perry at second. Bulldog Hershiser struck out Murphy three more times that day. After the third inning, the Braves went hitless for five innings. Orel shut out Atlanta 3–0.

On September 10, Hershiser faced the Cincinnati Reds, who had won eight of their last ten games. The games was scoreless in the third inning. Then, with the bases loaded, Eric Davis came up to bat. The last thing Orel wanted to do was give Davis a pitch he could hit over the fence. A home run would put the Reds ahead 4–0. But, with the bases loaded, Orel couldn't afford to walk Davis either. The batter got two strikes, and on the next pitch, Davis started to swing at the ball. He stopped before his bat crossed the plate. But the umpire called the swing a strike, and the inning was over.

By the seventh inning, Los Angeles led 3–0. But with just one out, Cincinnati again threatened to score by putting runners on first and third. Ken Griffey popped out, and then Hershiser struck out Barry Larkin to end the inning. The Dodgers finally won 5–0—Orel's second shutout in a row. Counting the last four innings against the Expos, he had pitched 22 straight scoreless innings.

Hershiser struck out Dale Murphy on his way to a shutout over the Atlanta Braves.

Hershiser and Atlanta's Rick Mahler had a great pitchers' duel on September 14. There was still no score in the seventh when Andres Thomas got a leadoff double for the Braves. Dion James followed with an easy grounder to first baseman Franklin Stubbs. Hershiser raced to first base to take the throw, but the ball went wide and he couldn't keep his foot on the bag. James was safe, and Thomas had moved to third. The next batter—Ozzie Virgil—also hit a grounder to Stubbs, who fielded it and made the play himself. The Braves now had one out with runners at second and third. Orel walked Jerry Blocker to load the bases. With the bases loaded it would be easier to get a double play and prevent the run from scoring. This strategy also brought up Mahler, the pitcher. Hershiser struck him out.

His next pitch was a curveball to Ron Gant, and Orel immediately knew it was a bad one. The ball was going in big and fat and slow. Gant pounded it into the outfield, and Dodger Kirk Gibson took off for the fence. Gibson caught the ball just before he hit the wall. The Braves were out, and Orel's scoreless innings streak stood at 29. When Atlanta's Mahler walked Gibson to start the bottom of the ninth, the game was still scoreless. Then Mike Marshall slammed the ball into the corner of left field. Gibson took off, not even slowing at third base. "No one was going to stop me," he said. Gibson scored to give Hershiser a 1–0 shutout victory. The streak was now 31 innings without a run!

The next day the Hershisers had something to think about besides scoreless innings and the pennant race. Jamie gave birth to their second son, Jordan Douglass, who was a very sick baby. Jordan's lungs were filled with fluid, and he was having trouble breathing. The Hershisers asked their friends to pray for their sick son. Orel stayed at the hospital with Jamie and Jordan when the Dodgers headed to Cincinnati for a game

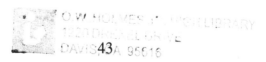
43

with the Reds. He told Tommy Lasorda he'd be back with the team when it was his turn to pitch. The manager agreed Orel should be with his family.

After three days Jordan began to improve. He was still a sick baby, but his lungs were stronger and he was going to live. By then it was time for his father to pitch against the Astros in Houston, Texas. Once again Orel knew he had a job to do. He was paid a lot of money to get batters out for the Dodgers, and that was what he was going to do.

When he rejoined the team, he told reporters that his son's condition had improved and that it was time to concentrate on baseball. But in the first inning his scoreless streak was in trouble. With two outs, Kevin Bass singled for the Astros. He stole second and then made it to third on an error. If Buddy Bell—the next batter—got a hit, Bass would easily score. Bell sent the ball into the outfield, but it was an easy fly ball. The first inning ended without a score.

Hershiser didn't have much more trouble with Houston—the Astros only got three more hits. But the Dodgers weren't hitting either. The game remained scoreless until Dodger John Shelby homered in the seventh. Orel had his second 1–0 victory in a row, and his streak stood at 40 innings!

Baseball fans were beginning to notice Orel's streak. Some of them thought Hershiser had a chance to break the major league record of 58 scoreless innings set by another Los Angeles pitcher, Don Drysdale, in 1968. Drysdale wished him luck. He said he was glad Orel was a Dodger.

Orel knew he still had a long way to go. Even if he pitched two more shutouts, he'd still be an inning away from breaking the record. He also kept reminding reporters that the important thing was that the Dodgers win the pennant, not that he break the record.

On September 23, Orel got himself into trouble against San Francisco. Giant player Jose Uribe singled to lead off the third inning. Atlee Hammaker tried to move his teammate to second with a sacrifice bunt. Hershiser fielded the ball, but he slipped and couldn't throw out Hammaker. So the Giants had two men on with no outs. Dodger third baseman Jeff Hamilton fielded Brett Butler's grounder and threw the ball to second. Hammaker was out this time, but Butler beat the throw to first. Now there were runners on first and third with only one out. The next batter was Ernest Riles. If he got a hit, or even hit a fly ball to the outfield, Uribe would score. Hershiser needed a strike out, an easy ground ball, or an infield pop out.

Riles hit a bouncing ball to second baseman Steve Sax, and Uribe took off for home. Sax decided to go for the double play. If the Dodgers got two outs on the play, Uribe's run wouldn't count. So Sax threw the ball to Alfredo Griffin, who touched second base for the force out on Butler. All Griffin had to do was get the ball to first to complete the double play. But Griffin's throw was wild, and Riles was safe. Uribe crossed the plate, and the Giants led 1–0. After 42 innings, Hershiser had finally given up a run—or at least that's the way it looked.

But as Will Clark walked up to the plate, second base umpire Paul Runge signaled that the inning was over. He said that Butler had gone out of the baseline and gotten in Griffin's way of throwing to first. Because Butler was called for interference, Riles was automatically out at first. With three outs, Uribe's run didn't count. The inning was over, and the streak went on! Hershiser ran for the dugout with a big smile on his face. He knew he had just gotten a very big break.

Orel shut out the Giants the rest of the day. His teammate Mickey Hatcher finally hit a three-run homer in the eighth inning. Los Angeles won 3–0, and the streak was up to 49 innings! Three days later the Dodgers clinched the Western Division title by beating San Diego 3–2. Now, as they waited for the regular season to end, Hershiser and his teammates could concentrate on the scoreless innings record.

Orel admitted he was excited about going for the record, but he knew it was going to be tough to break it in 1988. He had just one start left and he still needed ten innings to break the record. Even if he pitched a nine-inning shutout, he would only tie Drysdale's record. Since it was a regular season record, he'd have to wait until the 1989 season to break it.

The San Diego Padres wanted to make sure Hershiser didn't get that far. They were the Dodgers' opponent for his last regular season start. Tony Gwynn, the National League batting leader, looked forward to the challenge. He had studied video tapes of Hershiser pitching, so that he would be ready.

San Francisco's Jose Uribe thought he had scored the run that broke Hershiser's record.

But the game on September 28 belonged to Hershiser. Gwynn never got on base. He said Hershiser had never been tougher. Orel kept the Padres scoreless, but once again the Dodgers weren't scoring either. When Orel walked out to the mound for the seventh inning, he had only given up two hits. The San Diego fans surprised him by giving him a standing ovation. They knew he was closing in on the record. After he put the Padres down in order, he had 56 scoreless innings.

In the eighth inning, Roberto Alomar—a fast runner—singled for San Diego. When he took a big lead off first, the Dodgers were afraid he'd try to steal second base. Once Alomar got to second, he could score on a single. Orel didn't want to let that happen. After his first pitch to Tim Flannery, Orel fired the ball to first. Alomar was so far off the bag he couldn't get back in time. He was tagged out, and the inning was over.

The game was still scoreless, and for once the Dodgers' lack of runs might be helpful to Orel. If the game was tied after nine innings, it would go into extra innings. Then he would get a chance to break the record that night. In the top of the ninth, catcher Mike Scioscia asked Hershiser if he wanted him to hit a home run and end the game or just get a base hit so the game could continue. Hershiser laughed. In fact, the Dodgers failed to get a run or even a hit.

In the bottom of the ninth, the Padres were retired on three straight groundouts. Orel had 58 innings, and the game was still scoreless. He was going to get a chance to break the record. The crowd roared as the Dodgers welcomed him back to the dugout. Hershiser surprised Lasorda by asking to be taken out of the game. He said he wanted to break the record at Dodger Stadium the next season. Lasorda thought that idea was crazy. He told Orel he owed it to himself and the team to go for the record that night.

After the Dodgers failed to score, Orel walked back to the

mound. He looked toward Drysdale in the stands and tipped his cap. Padre Marvelle Wynne struck out, but the pitch got away from catcher Scioscia. So Wynne was safe at first base. Benito Santiago's sacrifice bunt and Randy Ready's ground out moved Wynne to third.

Hershiser decided to walk Garry Templeton intentionally to set up a force out at second. After his second ball, he was already thinking about pitching to the next batter. So he wasn't paying attention when Scioscia threw him the ball. By the time Orel saw the ball coming, it was almost too late. He lunged to the side and barely caught it before it sailed into center field. Hershiser and Wynne smiled at each other. They knew that if the throw had gotten past Orel, Wynne would've come home. The game and the streak would've been over. "I had so much pressure on me out there," Orel said after the game. "That's probably the most nervous I've ever been in my career."

Hershiser now had to focus his attention on Keith Moreland, the next batter. Moreland got two called strikes, then hit a foul ball. One more strike and the inning would be over. But if Moreland got a hit, Wynne would easily score, and the streak would be over. Wynne took a short lead off third as Orel fired a fastball. Moreland swung, and Wynne took off for home.

The ball flew over the infielders' heads, but it was a soft easy fly ball, heading straight to rightfielder Jose Gonzalez. He caught the ball easily, and the inning was over. Hershiser had pitched 59 consecutive scoreless innings! He now owned the record!

The Dodgers charged onto the field and mobbed Orel. Drysdale met him in the dugout and congratulated him. Then Lasorda pulled Hershiser out of the game. The Dodgers eventually lost in sixteen innings 2–1, but nobody seemed to

Don Drysdale watched Hershiser try to break his record of 58 consecutive scoreless innings.

care. The division title was already won, and Orel had broken the record. Now the Dodgers could concentrate on the New York Mets—the team they would face in the National League Championship Series.

Hershiser finished the season with 23 victories. This was the most for a Los Angeles pitcher since Sandy Koufax got 27 in 1966. Koufax had pitched with Drysdale and coached Hershiser in the minor leagues. "I was proud of Orel," Koufax said, "but a little sad for Don. It's an amazing record. . . . I can believe almost anything that happens in a single game, but such sustained excellence over such a long period with no margin for error, is unbelievable."

Chapter 6

During the 1988 regular season, the Mets had beaten the
Dodgers ten out of eleven times. If they won four more in the
championship series, they'd be in the World Series. In the first
game, Hershiser would be going against Dwight Gooden. The
Mets' pitcher was having a pretty good season himself with an
18–9 record. "I can't dwell on what Hershiser has done,"
Gooden said. "I'll have to let my hitters take care of him."

Instead it looked like Hershiser would be taking care of
the New York hitters. He blanked the Mets for eight innings.
Meanwhile Dodger Mike Marshall singled in Steve Sax in the
first inning. Mike Scioscia doubled in the seventh and then
scored on Alfredo Griffin's single. Going into the ninth, Los
Angeles led 2–0.

Gregg Jeffries opened the last inning with a single for
New York. Keith Hernandez grounded out, moving Jeffries to
second. The next batter was Darryl Strawberry. He knew the
Mets needed a hit. "That's part of my job," he said. "That's
what I'm out here to do. He gave me a pitch to hit, out over
the plate." It was a curveball that hung over the plate, and

Strawberry slammed it into center field. Jeffries scored, Strawberry wound up at second, and Orel had finally given up a run. Lasorda decided that was enough. Hershiser was replaced by reliever Jay Howell. The Dodgers still led 2–1, but there was only one out.

Howell walked Kevin McReynolds and struck out Howard Johnson. There were now two outs with runners on first and second. Howell got two quick strikes on Gary Carter. The next pitch was a good-looking curve. Carter connected with the ball, but broke his bat. The ball wobbled into short center field. John Shelby charged in, trying to make the catch. Strawberry and McReynolds took off for home. The ball was falling fast, and Shelby dove for it. But the ball bounced off his glove, allowing Strawberry to score. Shelby finally got the ball and threw it home. Scioscia blocked the plate, waiting for the ball. But McReynolds got home first, knocked Scioscia down, and scored the winning run. The Mets had a come-from-behind 3–2 victory.

After this disappointing opener, Los Angeles won 6–3. Then it was Hershiser's turn to play again. The game was tied when he was finally pulled for a pinch hitter in the eighth inning. Mike Sharperson walked with the bases loaded, giving Los Angeles a 4–3 lead. Then the Mets exploded for five runs in their half of the eighth and won 8–4. Hershiser had pitched two games, and the Dodgers had failed to win either one. Los Angeles trailed in the series 2–1.

In the ninth inning of the fourth game, New York led 4–2. Shelby walked, and Scioscia homered to tie up the game. There was no more scoring until the twelfth when Kirk Gibson crashed a solo home run. The Dodgers now had a 5–4 lead.

Then Mickey Sasser and Lee Mazilli singled for the Mets. After Tim Leary got Jeffries to fly out, Lasorda replaced him

After Darryl Strawberry's hit, Lasorda took Hershiser out of the first game of the 1988 National League Championship Series. Later Strawberry and Hershiser were teammates on the Dodgers.

with relief pitcher Jesse Orosco. Orosco walked Hernandez to load the bases. Meanwhile in the bull pen, Hershiser began to warm up. He wanted to help the team any way he could. If that meant being a relief pitcher again, he'd do it.

Orosco got the second out of the inning when Strawberry popped up and the runners held. "I'm bringing in the Bulldog," Lasorda said. "I'm putting the pot of gold on the Bulldog." Almost all the rest of his pitchers had already seen action in this long game. There was nobody else left. It was a pressure-packed situation: tie game, bases loaded, two outs, in the bottom of the twelfth. If Hershiser couldn't hold the Mets, Los Angeles would be down three games to one.

McReynolds took a strike, then watched a ball go by. Orel's next pitch was a sinking fastball. McReynolds hit a weak fly into center field. It looked like the same ball Carter had hit to win the first game. Once again Shelby charged in with all the runners moving. At the last instant Shelby leaned forward and made a running catch. The Dodgers had won the game and tied the series!

After the teams split the next two games, the stage was set for a dramatic seventh-game showdown. For once, the Dodgers were hitting, and after just two innings, they led 6–0. Orel allowed only five hits and cruised to a win. The game ended when he struck out Johnson with a fastball. Just before he was mobbed by his teammates, Orel dropped to one knee and said a quick prayer of thanks. That action made his mother happy. "That's my favorite moment of the year," she said. "At a time like that, he remembered to thank God."

But, of course, the season wasn't over yet. Hershiser and the Dodgers had to face the Oakland A's in the World Series. Gibson's ninth inning home run won the opening game. Then Orel's two victories helped give Los Angeles the title.

Orel didn't mind coming in as a relief pitcher when the Dodgers needed him against the Mets.

The year 1988 was incredible for Hershiser. His team had won it all. He was awarded the MVP Award in the Championship Series and the World Series. He took the Cy Young Award as the finest pitcher in the National League. *Sports Illustrated* named him "Sportsman of the Year." When the season was over, he and the Dodgers signed an agreement. The contract made him the highest-paid player in baseball. Over the next three years, he would be paid almost eight million dollars!

Hershiser didn't enjoy the same level of success in 1989. Even though he had an ERA of 2.31, his record sank to 15–15. During his fifteen losses, the Dodgers scored only seventeen runs. Orel had lost seven games in a row before he finally pitched eleven innings and won his last game of the year.

The year 1990 proved an even rougher season for Orel. He only started four games, and many people thought his baseball career was over. Just before spring training he noticed something was wrong with his arm. When he reached to point or grab something with his right hand, he said, "my shoulder would click and would feel like it was popping out of the socket." After he began pitching regularly, his shoulder really started to hurt. The pain got so bad that it was hard for him to throw the ball. On April 25, he gave up three walks and four runs in one inning against the St. Louis Cardinals. "I knew I was hurting the team as bad as I was hurting myself."

The Dodgers sent him to the hospital to have his shoulder examined. "Orel, I'm afraid this is very serious," the doctor told him. "We're talking about surgery here. We're talking about a year rehab. We're talking about never making it back." Orel was shocked. He had pitched 195 games without missing his turn in the starting rotation. He couldn't believe there was a chance he would never pitch again.

The doctor explained to Hershiser that every time he

pitched his shoulder had slipped just a bit out of joint and then popped back into place. After thousands of pitches, the soft tissue around the joint was badly damaged. On April 27, doctors made a four-and-a-half inch incision in Orel's shoulder. They shortened the tendons that held his muscles to the bones of his shoulder. Then they fastened the tendons to new spots on the bones. The purpose of the operation was to tighten the shoulder joint, so that he could pitch again. But nobody was sure the procedure would work.

Orel spent the rest of the 1990 season massaging, stretching, and exercising his shoulder. He worked hard to get back in shape because, he said, "I love the game. I love to compete." Sometimes he was frustrated because the shoulder joint was so stiff and sore he could barely move it. But he kept working out every day. The only good that came out of the injury was that he got to spend a lot of time with his family. Each night before his sons went to bed they prayed, "God, please help Daddy's shoulder."

Lasorda never doubted that his star pitcher would be back. "If anybody could come back from this type of injury, it's the Bulldog," he said. "I know his intensity. I know his desire."

After the operation it took Orel a year to get back on the mound. His first start was May 8, 1991, for the Bakersfield Dodgers—a Class A minor league team. He pitched five shutout innings and only allowed two hits. "It was a lot of fun to be back on the mound and feel that adrenaline again," he said. "My arm is moving again in a way I can pitch." After the game he didn't go home until he had signed autographs for more than 100 fans who had waited outside the stadium.

Hershiser pitched in three more minor league games before Lasorda and the doctors decided he was again ready for the major leagues. It wasn't until May 29 that Hershiser pitched his first game of the 1991 season. The fans cheered

Doctors told Orel there was a chance he would never pitch again.

hard and long, and Orel almost cried. But the Houston Astros bombed him for four runs in the first inning. After that Orel settled down. "Since that first inning, he's been dazzling," said Scioscia. "A healthy Orel Hershiser is a tremendous pitcher, and that's given us a big lift."

In 1991 Los Angeles finished one game behind the Atlanta Braves in the National League West. Hershiser went 7–2 with an ERA of 3.46. After the season he signed another contract with the Dodgers—this one for ten million dollars over three years! The contract meant that if Orel remained healthy, he'd be playing in Los Angeles at least through the end of the 1994 season. This was great news for Dodger fans who were anxious for another World Series title. And it was great news for sports fans in general.

Orel did return to the World Series—but not with the Dodgers. After twelve years with the Dodgers, Orel took to the mound in a Cleveland Indians uniform on April 16, 1995. He had signed a one-year, $1.45 million contract with the Indians on April 8. The deal included a $1.5 million club option for 1996. When asked about the change, Orel said, "Same thing in an Indians uniform as a Dodgers uniform. It's still 60 feet, 6 inches to the plate, still 90 feet to first. Still playing with a bunch of great guys."

Great and talented guys—the Indians made their way to the World Series in 1995, only to lose to the Atlanta Braves, 4 games to 2. At age thirty-six, Orel went 1–1 in the Series for a combined 20–7 record during the regular and postseason.

Hershiser had another solid year for the Indians in 1996, finishing with a record of 15–9. The Indians finished first in their division once again, but fell to the Baltimore Orioles in the division semifinals 3 games to 1. Even at this stage of his career, Hershiser continues to be a major threat to opposing hitters.

Career Statistics

Year	Team	W	L	G	IP	H	R	ER	BB	SO	ER/
1979	Clinton*	4	0	15	43	33	15	10	17	33	2.0
1980	San Antonio*	5	9	49	109	120	59	43	59	75	3.5
1981	San Antonio*	7	6	42	102	94	54	53	50	95	4.6
1982	Albuquerque*	9	6	47	12.6	121	73	51	63	93	3.7
1983	Albuquerque*	10	8	49	134.3	132	73	61	57	95	4.0
	Los Angeles	0	0	8	8	7	6	3	6	5	3.3
1984	Los Angeles	11	8	45	189.6	160	65	56	50	150	2.6
1985	Los Angeles	19	3	36	239.6	179	72	54	68	157	2.0
1986	Los Angeles	14	14	35	231.3	213	112	99	86	153	3.8
1987	Los Angeles	16	16	37	264.6	247	105	90	74	190	3.0
1988	Los Angeles	23	8	35	267	208	73	67	73	178	2.2
1989	Los Angeles	15	15	35	256.6	226	75	66	77	178	2.3
1990	Los Angeles	1	1	4	25.3	26	12	12	4	16	4.2
1991	Los Angeles	7	2	21	34	112	43	43	32	73	3.4
1992	Los Angeles	10	15	33	210.6	209	101	86	69	130	3.6
1993	Los Angeles	12	14	33	215.6	201	106	86	72	141	3.5
1994	Los Angeles	6	6	21	135.3	146	67	57	42	72	3.7
1995	Cleveland	16	6	26	167.3	151	76	72	51	111	3.8
1996	Cleveland	15	9	33	206	238	115	97	58	125	4.2
Major League Total		165	117	402	2,451.3	2,323	1,028	888	762	1,679	3.1

* Minor Leagu

Where to Write Orel Hershiser:

Mr. Orel Hershiser
c/o Cleveland Indians
Jacobs Field
2401 Ontario Street
Cleveland, OH 44115

Index

A

Adray Appliance, 18
Albuquerque Dodgers, 22, 25, 27, 29
All American Amateur Baseball Association, 18
Alomar, Roberto, 47
appendix, 36, 38, 39
Arizona Instructional League, 22, 24
Atlanta Braves, 32, 41, 43, 59

B

Babe Ruth League, 17
Bakersfield Dodgers, 57
Bartley, Boyd, 21
Bass, Kevin, 44
Bell, Buddy, 44
Bible, 24
Blocker, Jerry, 43
Bowling Green University, 17–18, 21
Buffalo, New York, 14, 16
"Bulldog," 29
Butler, Brett, 45

C

Canseco, Jose, 9
Carter, Gary, 52, 54
Cherry Hill High School, 17
Cherry Hill, New Jersey, 16–17
Cherry Hill News, 17
Chicago Cubs, 32

christianity, 24
Cincinnati Reds, 32, 41, 43–44
Clark, Will, 45
Clinton Dodgers, 21, 22, 24
Cy Young Award, 56

D

Davis, Eric, 41
Davis, Mike, 36
Dearie Mulvey Award, 27
Dempsey, Rick, 9
Dodger Stadium, 34, 47
Drysdale, Don, 44, 48, 50

E

El Paso, Texas, 25
Esasky, Nick, 32

G

Gant, Ron, 43
Gibson, Kirk, 13, 36, 43, 52
Gonzalez, Jose, 48
Gooden Dwight, 51
Griffey, Ken, 41
Griffin, Alfredo, 7, 45, 51
Gwynn, Tony, 34, 46–47

H

Hamilton, Jeff, 45
Hammaker, Atlee, 45
Hassey, Ron, 11
Hatcher, Mickey, 7, 45
Henderson, Rickey, 9

Hernandez, Keith, 51, 54
Hershiser, Gordie, 16, 38
Hershiser, Jamie, 11, 24–25, 27,
    34, 36, 38, 43–44, 57
Hershiser, Jordan Douglass,
    43–44, 57
Hershiser, Judd, 16
Hershiser, Katie, 16
Hershiser, Millie, 14, 54
Hershiser, Orel I, 34
Hershiser, Orel II, 34
Hershiser, Orel III, 14, 34
Hershiser, Orel V "Quinton,"
    34, 57
Houston Astros, 44
Howell, Jay, 52

I
ice hockey, 16–17

J
James, Dion, 43
Javier, Stan, 9
Jeffries, Gregg, 51, 52
Johnson, Howard, 52, 54

K
Kent State University, 18, 21
Koufax, Sandy, 50

L
Lansford, Carney, 9, 11
Lasorda, Tommy, 9, 27, 29, 30,
    32, 44, 47, 48, 52, 54,
    57, 59
Leary, Tim, 52
Little League, 16
Los Angeles Dodgers, 7–9, 11,
    13, 21, 23, 25–59

M
Mahler, Rick, 43
Marshall Mike, 43, 51
Martinez, Davey, 41
Mazilli, Lee, 52
McGwire, Mark, 11
McReynolds, Kevin, 52, 54
Montreal Expos, 41
Moreland, Keith, 48
Murphy, Dale, 32, 41

N
National League Championship
    Series, 50, 51–56
National League Pitcher of the
    Month, 39
New York City, 15
New York Mets, 30, 32, 50,
    51–55

O
Oakland Athletics, 7–11
Oakland Coliseum, 7
Orosco, Jesse, 54

P
Parker, Dave, 7, 11
Perranoski, Ron, 30
Perry, Gerald, 41
Personna Baseball Contest, 15
Philadelphia Flyers, 17
Phillips, Tony, 9, 11
Pittsburgh Pirates, 32, 39

R
Raines, Tim, 41
Reuss, Jerry, 30, 32
Riles, Ernest, 45
Runge, Paul, 45

S

San Antonio Dodgers, 22, 24–25
San Diego Padres, 34–36, 46–48
San Francisco Giants, 30, 39, 45
Santiago, Benito, 48
Sasser, Mickey, 52
Sax, Steve, 45, 51
Scioscia, Mike, 47, 48, 51, 52, 59
Sharperson, Mike, 52
Shelby, John, 11, 44, 52, 54
Southfield, Michigan, 14–16
Sports Illustrated, 56
"Sportsman of the Year," 56
St. Louis Cardinals, 32, 56
Strawberry, Darryl, 51–52, 54
Stubbs, Franklin, 7, 43

T

tee ball, 14
Templeton, Garry, 48
Texas League, 25
Texas Rangers, 25
Thomas, Andres, 43
Toronto, Canada, 16

U

Uribe, Jose, 45

V

Virgil, Ozzie, 43

W

Wickensheimer, Butch, 24
World Series, 7–13, 54, 56, 59
Wynne, Marvelle, 48

Y

Yankee Stadium, 15–16, 21